from:
frank™

DON'T FART
WHEN YOU SNUGGLE.

Lessons on how to make a human smile.

CHRONICLE BOOKS
SAN FRANCISCO

Library of Congress Cataloging-in-Publication Date
is available.
ISBN: 978-1-4521-4177-0

Manufactured in China

10 9 8 7 6 5 4 3 2 1

Chronicle Books LLC
680 Second Street
San Francisco, California 94107
www.chroniclebooks.com

DEDICATION:

To humans.
(And that hot poodle down
the street...call me.)

WE ALL KNOW HUMANS
LOVE TO SMILE.

And we love helping them do it. But for some, this
skill just doesn't come as naturally as it does
for others. Don't worry, that's where I come in.
Making humans smile is my mission in life. It's my
thing. And I'm really, really good at it. So, I've
gathered up my best friends and together we have
compiled our most tried and true tips, tricks,
and advice for making humans happy.
Follow our advice and you're
in for some extra belly
rubs, guaranteed.

You're Welcome,
Frank

HI. I'M FRANK.

I guess you could say I'm a bit of a leader. I've got big ideas and I've always preferred the front of the pack. And my favorite perk of being an alpha dog? The ladies. They love me. I mean, who wouldn't, right? And as much as they try to get me to settle down, I always prefer to keep my options open.

MEET WALTER.

My oldest friend – in age and in time. Walter has been around the block a few times and loves reminiscing about the days when the ladies flocked to him. Age has made him wise. And amid his snide, sometimes inappropriate remarks, you'll probably learn something.

MEET BIG LOUIE.

My brother from another mother.
Big Louie has never met a
shortcut he didn't want to take.
He is slow, chubby, and sloppy,
but he has a big heart. He may
not always know the right thing
to do, and may be sleeping when
it's time to do it, but Big Louie
tries and that's what makes
him so lovable.

MEET LULU MCFLUFF.

My optimist friend. Lulu is a happy-go-lucky fluff-ball wearing rose-colored glasses so thick that she's also a bit clueless. Lulu always sees the bright side, even when her bright side may not seem so appealing to anyone else.

MEET IZZY.

My realist friend. Izzy has always been more of a "dog's girl" and tends to get along better with us than cats. We're okay with that. We like her because she's always up for some mischief, and you can be sure she'll tell you if you look fat in that collar.

GREETINGS

I don't think I've ever had a bad greeting. They always make humans smile.

Yes. My rule is see a human, greet a human.

That seems like a lot of effort. All that getting up...

Everything is a lot of effort for you, Louie.

So, what if they just went out to the back yard and came back in?

Greeting.

What if they just went to another room in the house?

Greeting.

What if they just put a blanket over their head and take it back off?

Benefit of the doubt. Greeting.

7:00 a.m.

9:25 a.m.

GREET YOUR HUMAN LIKE
IT'S THE FIRST TIME...

EVERY TIME.

8:56 p.m.

5:10 p.m.

11:25 p.m.

GREET YOUR HUMAN
WHEN THEY WAKE UP...

HUMPING IS NOT HELLO.

Let them tell you about their day first.

HUMPING
APPRECIATION GUIDE

Humping is a very delicate technique.
Some humans find it hilarious and others
just down right offensive (weird,
I know). Use this guide to gauge your
audience and increase your chances of
success before your next hump.

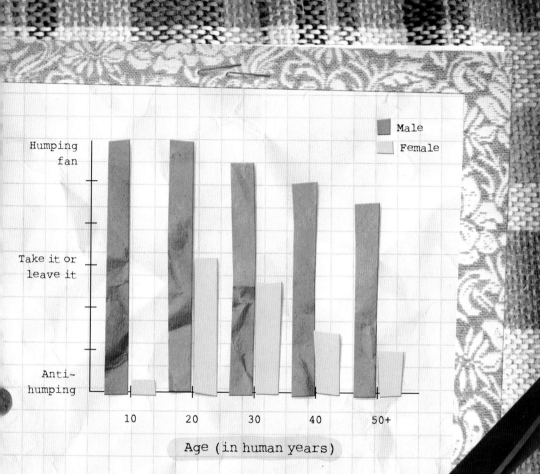

GREET YOUR HUMAN WITH A SMILE.

Especially if you've just pooped in the other room.

SHAKE THEIR HAND.

Being formal feels fancy.

SHOW THEM YOUR BELLY.

Peeing during this time
is not recommended.

SNIFF ANY GUEST CROTCHES.

As head of household security,
it's a necessary precaution.

INVESTIGATE ANY UNIDENTIFIED OBJECTS.

You never know where you'll find a treat.

LEAVE NO LEG UNRUBBED.

The hair you leave behind shows humans
that they have been properly greeted.

INTRODUCE YOUR HUMAN TO OTHERS ON WALKS.

Humans like to make friends and sometimes just need an icebreaker.

Icebreaker techniques to try:

- Show them your belly.

- Make your body go totally limp right in their walking path.

- Incessant barking.

- Pee on another dog.

- Hump another dog.

- Hump a human.

GREET FIRST.
THEN ASK ABOUT DINNER.

Not vice versa.

THE MORE CIRCLES YOU TURN THE BETTER THE GREETING.

You may get dizzy...and need to lay down.

CHEER LOUDLY FOR YOUR HUMAN.

Everyone loves a personal pep rally.

PERFECT YOUR
BUTT WIGGLE.

There's no such thing as
too much butt wiggle.

WATER BOWL TALK.

SHOWING AFFECTION

We all know humans love gifts. So, favorite gift to give your human. Go...

I'd say, bring them their slippers.

Wow. How original.

Oh, and what amazing gift do you give humans?

My presence.
It is truly a gift.

Exactly. I'm pretty sure you've never given a gift in your life.

I mean, I do enjoy Izzy's presence.

She does leave delicious little gifts in her litter box everyday...

Oh, yes, that's true...

Those are delicious.

...I know.

HUMANS LOVE GIFTS.

Just make sure it's not dead
or regurgitated.

Good gifts:

- Today's newspaper
- Bone
- Slippers
- Snuggles
- High five
- Your food bowl

Bad gifts:

- Newspaper from 2 days ago (regurgitated)
- Dead bug
- Chewed slippers
- Cat turd
- House plant (that you stole from the other room)

CHASE YOUR TAIL.

This is fun for humans.
Act like you don't know it's on your butt.

ENCOURAGE SLEEPING IN.

What's so important, anyway?

LAY ON YOUR HUMAN'S CLOTHES.

- Your smell makes them feel close to you when they're away.

- Stray hairs on clothing show your human has a pet and who doesn't want to show that off to other humans?

- Clothes warmed by your butt have a more personal touch than clothes warmed by the dryer.

- Wrinkles give a nice texture to their look.

- When else would they get to use that fun sticky lint roller?

DON'T EAT THEIR SOCKS...

THE CLOSER YOU CAN GET TO THE HUMAN THE BETTER YOU CAN LOVE THEM.

Avoid sneezing when this close.

GIVE IN TO THE BATH.

Everyone needs their wiener
washed once in a while.

HELP OUT IN THE KITCHEN.

Those dirty plates aren't going
to lick themselves.

RESIST THE URGE TO MARK YOUR HUMAN.

They know you love them without pee on their leg.

ALWAYS SNIFF THEIR BUTT.

Passing over would be very
offensive to the human.

LET THEM
DRESS YOU UP.

It brings them joy.

HYDRANT.

I was peed on...twice.

DINOSAUR.

They're extinct for a reason.

PRINCESS.

I'm not gonna lie. I feel pretty.

BACON.

I really thought this costume
came with bacon.

JAILBIRD.

The only crime is this outfit.

Bored face

Serious face

HUMANS LOVE PHOTOS.
DON'T FIGHT IT.

Develop some different poses and faces to give them options.

Sexy face

Happy face

Tired face

WALK YOUR HUMAN DAILY.

It's good for them and you can check out that hot poodle down the street.

DRIP YOUR WATER ON THE FLOOR.

It reminds your human to drink more water themselves.

HAVE A BALL.

In fact, have 12. Humans love searching for tennis balls.

INSIST ON BELLY RUBS.

Have you ever seen an
unhappy belly-rubber?

ALWAYS FILL
AN EMPTY LAP.

One size fits all.

WATER BOWL TALK.

SNUGGLING

Snuggling is a no-brainer tip to make humans smile. They can't get enough.

You have to admit, there is a point where it gets awkward.

One time I snuggled with someone for 8 hours straight.

No, you didn't.

You were sleeping and the person was watching a TV marathon.

It's true, Louie. Touching is not snuggling.

At least Big Louie isn't a creepy snuggler like Izzy.

What? People love my constant, direct eye contact while snuggling.

It's creepy.

...it is creepy.

ARMPITTING IS
THE NEW SPOONING.

THERE IS SUCH A THING
AS TOO COMFORTABLE.

USE THE PAW TOUCH.

It's the polite way to snuggle humans
with personal space issues.

DON'T FART
WHEN YOU SNUGGLE.

Surprisingly, humans are not big fans.

DON'T BE THE BIG SPOON...

...if you're really the little spoon.

EASY WITH THE CLAWS.

Nobody likes snuggle marks.

KEEP YOUR BREATH FRESH.

Eat the cat turd after
snuggling...not before.

CHOOSING YOUR SNUGGLE TECHNIQUE.

Does your mind get boggled trying to decide what kind of a snuggle your human wants? Are you always getting it wrong? Well, this cheat sheet is for you. Your human will think you're a snuggle mind reader.

Nose snuggle:

This technique is simple and great for humans on the go. Just smoosh your nose to their nose and wiggle for a quick, satisfying mini-snuggle.

2 Feet snuggle:

This technique is great for preoccupied humans. Sometimes they get busy and forget to snuggle, so remind them by sitting on their feet. Hands-free snuggling at its finest.

3 Lap snuggle:

This technique is a classic and all-time human favorite. It can be done anywhere and there's usually petting involved. Win-win.

4 Full-on snuggle:

This technique is the real deal. Horizontal, blanket covered, mouth-open, drool-spot snuggling. Great for weekends.

THE LOUDER THE SNORE
THE BETTER THE SNUGGLE.

LICK THE HUMAN
WHEN SNUGGLING...

...NOT YOURSELF.

LICKING YOUR HUMAN.

A guide to the do's and don'ts:
(As shown on our stuffed monkey, Fred.)

Yes

Yes

N/A

(Humans don't
have tails.)

Yes

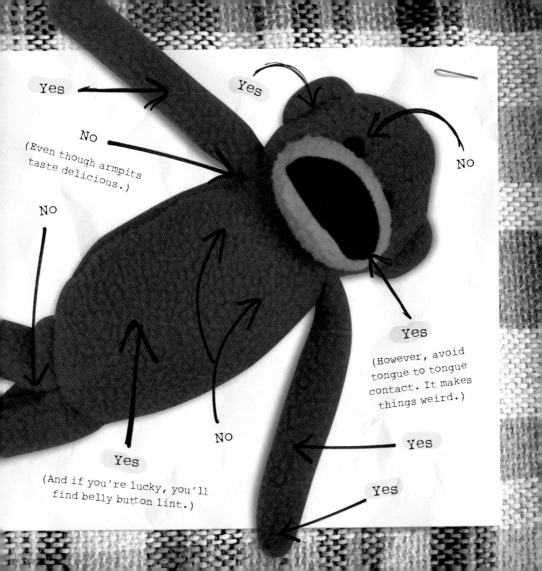

KNEAD YOUR HUMAN...
LITERALLY.

DON'T BE A COVER HOG.

GET ON BOARD WITH BEING HELD LIKE A BABY.

It's actually pretty spectacular.

SIT ON THEIR FEET...

...NOT THEIR HEAD.

IT'S 5 O'CLOCK SOMEWHERE.

There's never a bad time to snuggle.

	6 AM	Hit the snooze button snuggle.
	7 AM	Good morning snuggle.
	8 AM	Breakfast snuggle.
	9 AM	Post-shower snuggle. (Just as important as personal hygiene.)
	10 AM	Brunch snuggle.
	11 AM	Mid-morning break snuggle.
	12 PM	Lunch snuggle.

1 PM   After lunch nap snuggle.

2 PM   Post-nap snuggle.

3 PM   Mid-afternoon snuggle. (Recharge for the evening.)

4 PM   Snack snuggle.

5 PM   Happy hour snuggle. (Pre-game it for the dinner snuggle.)

6 PM   Dinner snuggle.

7 PM   Game show snuggle.

8 PM   Reality TV snuggle.

9 PM   Pre-sleep snuggle.

10 PM   You're sleeping. (Who doesn't want to snuggle?)

SNUGGLE FACE TO FACE.

Butt to face hasn't proven
very successful.

CONSTANT EYE CONTACT ISN'T DREAMY.

It's creepy.

WATER BOWL TALK.

QUIRKS

One of the most cutting-edge ways to make humans smile is quirks.

What's a quirk?

It's like things you do that are weird, but funny to humans at the same time.

I'm pretty sure a quirk is that brown thing that goes in a wine bottle.

Um...that's a cork.

A quirk is Frank fluffing his bed into the shape of a taco every night.

I fully stand behind the comfort of my taco beds.

So like when I spin in circles when I see a squirrel?

Exactly.

Or like when you have a bottle of wine and you want to keep it fresh?

No.

TREAT YOURSELF.

Give your human a break and get your own treats for once.

HIDE IN UNEXPECTED PLACES.

Humans love a good surprise.

KEEP FETCH FRESH.

Chase after the ball but bring back
something entirely different.

Ball retrieval alternatives:

- Hose
- Potted plant
- Random toy
- Grill brush
- Decorative rock
- Sprinkler (even better
  if it's still on)
- Tree branch

REMEMBER TO LOOK ADORABLE WHILE YOU SLEEP.

Stuffed animals help.

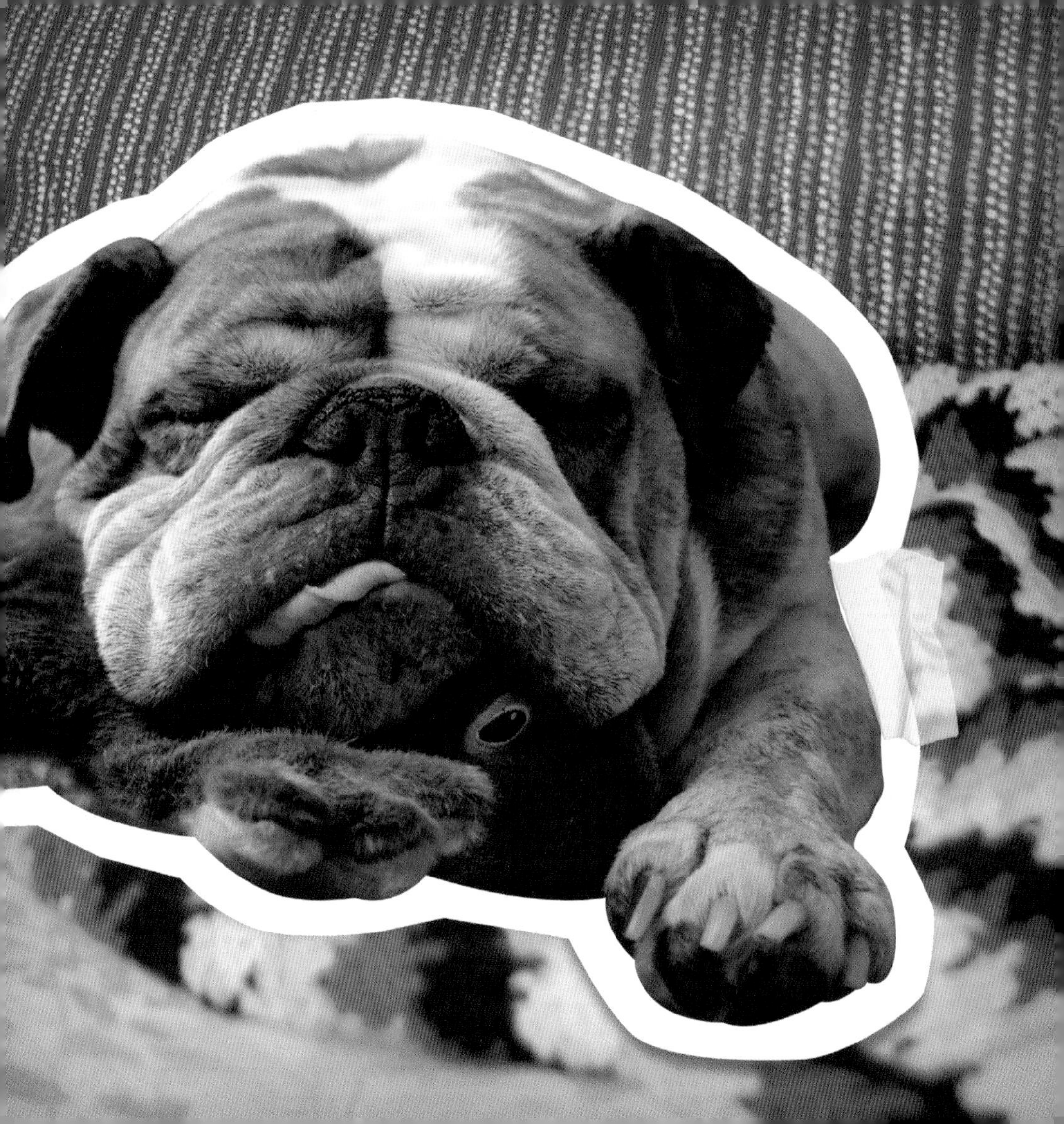

Miss Fuzzy Pants

Squeezy Cheeks

LET YOUR HUMAN CALL YOU FUNNY NAMES.

What they find endearing will most likely be embarrassing.

Stinky Butt

Fluffy McGee

Captain Sniffy

DON'T HAVE A NICKNAME?

Help your human out and create your own. Combine a word from the first column with a word from the second and voilà! Instant nickname magic.

1
- Fuzzy
- Stinky
- Squeezy
- Grumpy
- Fluffy
- Hairy
- Snorty
- Farty
- Fatty
- Sniffy

2
- Butt
- Face
- Cheeks
- McGee
- Sniffer
- Joe
- Paws
- Pants
- Bucket
- Tail

A word from here **+** A word from here **=** Your new nickname!

MARK · YOUR NEIGHBORHOOD...

Your utter domination and bladder control will impress your human.

...JUST AVOID YOUR PAWS.

Nobody likes to smell pee-paws. Nobody.

SLOW YOUR ROLL.

Unfortunately, humans don't appreciate the finer smells in life (We know...they're totally missing out). So, as a rule of thumb, if it smells amazing...you probably shouldn't roll on it. (Sorry.)

Don't roll:*

- On cat turds
- On raccoon poop
- On dead birds
- On trash

* Unless human is not watching.

ALWAYS FIT IN.

PROTECT YOUR HUMAN FROM THE MAILMAN.

Unless they have treats...
then all bets are off.

PREHEAT THE BATHROOM TILE.

Just don't get roped into the bath.

SAY YOU'RE SORRY.

(Even if you're not.)

FIND THE SUNNY SPOT.

And share it with your human.
(Sometimes.)

BLOW BUBBLES IN YOUR WATER BOWL.

Who doesn't love bubbles?

TURN BAD HABITS INTO ENTERTAINMENT.

Make your human laugh and watch discipline fly out the window.

Examples of brilliant naughtiness:

- Put every blanket and pillow in the house on the floor...literally every single one.

- Hug the toilet with all four legs while drinking from it.

- Shred your stuffed animals so fast that they give you another and get out a stop watch.

SLEEP IN CREATIVE WAYS...

Bridge pose.

...TO INSPIRE MORE NAPS FROM YOUR HUMAN.

Sitting-up pose.

MAKE THEIR BUSINESS,
YOUR BUSINESS.

Sitting on their work
improves productivity.

EVERY SO OFTEN,
BARK AT NOTHING.

Your human will feel extra protected.

WATER BOWL TALK.

WRAP-UP

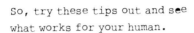

So, try these tips out and see what works for your human.

Yep, everyone's human is different. If you fail at one technique just try another.

Right, there's no shame in failing.

Isn't that Big Louie's life motto?

I don't know...trying things and failing at them means he would actually have to be awake.

Is he still sleeping?

Someone poke him.

No, wait, plug
his nose holes.

. . .

Or we could cover
him with tennis balls
like yesterday.

Nah, Let him sleep.
We've got humans to make
smile. And so do you.
Good luck my friends!

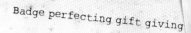

Badge perfecting gift giving

HOW DO YOU MAKE
YOUR HUMAN SMILE?

Show us how these tips worked for you or
even some techniques you've invented on
your own! #makinghumanssmile

Learn more about Frank, his friends and
their mission to make humans smile at
www.greetingsfromfrank.com

Tootsie nailing some constant, direct eye contact.

Peanut trying not to fart while snuggling.

Munchy's favorite way to make humans smile: We